EVEN MORE OFFENSIVE MARKETING

Hugh Davidson

> This 'Penguin 60' contains Dr Tony O'Reilly's Foreword to *Even More Offensive Marketing*, a 'Bulletin Board' describing the road map of the book, and a slightly abridged version of Chapter 1.
>
> Because of space limitations, there are no notes or references in this Penguin 60.
>
> *Even More Offensive Marketing*, by Hugh Davidson, is published by Penguin Business, and, from 2 October 1997, will be widely available in bookshops and at airports, priced at £12.99 (608 pages).

Penguin Books

PENGUIN BOOKS

Published by the Penguin Group

Penguin Books Ltd, 27 Wrights Lane, London W8 5TZ, England
Penguin Books USA Inc., 375 Hudson Street, New York, New York 10014, USA
Penguin Books Australia Ltd, Ringwood, Victoria, Australia
Penguin Books Canada Ltd, 10 Alcorn Avenue, Toronto, Ontario, Canada M4V 3B2
Penguin Books (NZ) Ltd, 182–190 Wairau Road, Auckland 10, New Zealand

Penguin Books Ltd, Registered Offices: Harmondsworth, Middlesex, England

This extract is taken from *Even More Offensive Marketing*, to be published in
Penguin Books in October 1997

1 3 5 7 9 10 8 6 4 2

Copyright © Hugh Davidson, 1997
All rights reserved

The moral right of the author has been asserted

Filmset in Bembo and Gill Sans

Printed in England by Clays Ltd, St Ives plc

Foreword

By Dr Anthony J. F. O'Reilly

Chairman, President and Chief Executive Officer
H. J. Heinz Co., Inc.

Chairman
Waterford Wedgwood

Since Hugh Davidson and I first collaborated in
1971, on the threshold of my US career with
H. J. Heinz, much has happened to both of us. Our
original collaboration was on *Offensive Marketing*,
which proved to be a bestseller. *Even More Offensive
Marketing* is its sequel. It retains the enduring
principles of the original, takes their application
forward beyond the millennium, and is a new book,
not a new edition.

Hugh Davidson is an iconoclast. He is also an
immensely readable writer, with a strong commercial sense. The strategy of his book underlines the
belief that successful marketing, or, in his view,
Offensive Marketing, comprises certain attitudes and
practices towards marketing, competition and planning which are, unfortunately, rare.

The rapid rate of marketing change has further
accelerated in the past five years. One aspect is 3

the development of Relationship Marketing. This involves an individual and long-term approach to customers, and has been of particular importance to both H. J. Heinz and Waterford Wedgwood. However, new product and brand development, appropriate investment in efficiency, technology and communication, and commitment to quality, value and service, remain critical to future marketing success.

Good marketing practice is based on freedom of consumer choice, which is an essential element in a democracy. Supermarkets are a better model of the democratic process in action than Congress or the Houses of Parliament. Customers impose their will on the producer and retailer by exercising their right to make choices in a competitive market. Hugh Davidson's book highlights the process of co-operation between consumer and producer and illustrates how mutual responsiveness can benefit both.

His definitions are refreshing and simple. He believes that professional marketing involves a determination to achieve all the major innovations in a given market, a freedom from the shackles of industry tradition or interruptive bureaucracy, and a view of marketing as a profit-oriented approach to business that permeates not just the Marketing

Department, but the entire business. Above all, he believes that Offensive Marketing requires a dedication to strategy and planning.

Hurray! It has all been said before, but it has rarely been said so succinctly and so refreshingly. Not above employing popular gurus to bolster his case, he quotes Levitt tellingly: 'When it comes to the marketing concept today, a solid stone wall often seems to separate word from deed.' His answer is, 'Kill the bureaucratic plague; dis-establish the maintenance men; stop talking about Offensive Marketing and DO something about it.' He observes, in my view accurately, that good marketing is not so much a matter of intelligence and ability (as good and bad companies seem to have an abundance of both), but more a question of attitudes, organization and technique.

Hugh Davidson has a certain elegance in his choice of mnemonics. He says that Offensive Marketing is a matter of POISE, that it should be Profitable, Offensive, Integrated, Strategic (embracing short- and long-term corporate plans) and Effectively Executed. The book unashamedly assumes that the right attitudes and organization structures have a profound effect on corporate profit, and essays only one real definition of marketing (and a very good 5 one it is), that it 'involves every employee in building superior customer value very efficiently for above-average profits'. He also stresses that if you don't balance the short-term-profit/consumer-benefit equation against your long-term ambitions, you won't have a business to realize those long-term ambitions against.

Offensive Marketing is quite simple to describe. A company's offerings must be so attractive to customers that they will want to buy and go on buying. The offerings must also be developed and marketed so efficiently that the company will make handsome profits. To succeed, both sides of the equation have to be matched. Good customer value or low-cost operation on their own are not enough in today's very competitive market-place.

The only way I know of achieving this simple formula is to have winning strategies, and strong well-motivated people to execute them. In Chapter 7 Davidson explains how to develop winning strategies. He also warns that they wear out quickly unless they are updated to meet changing customer needs and new competitive moves. The world is full of lagging companies which used to have winning strategies. I am a strong believer in the importance of attitudes and was glad to see a whole chapter devoted to this. Qualities we encourage at Heinz are ingenuity, dedication, willingness to chance risk and ability to spot a problem and pursue it doggedly. Talking about corporate culture is much easier than creating or sustaining it. From hard experience, I know that 'making it happen' requires example, emphasis and evangelism from all managers every day of the week.

What Davidson wants is integrated marketing, believing that it is an approach to business rather than a specific discipline. He states that the main benefits which successful companies gain through Offensive Marketing are higher profits, a longer life cycle on existing products and services, and a better success rate with new products and acquisitions. Could we ask for more?

My own experience suggests general accord with these principles, and great difficulty in implementing them. In particular, it is extremely difficult to graft policies of innovation and imagination on to big, successful organizations. The entrepreneur, by definition, is almost a loner. Large businesses have a certain civil-service-like quality about them. Promotion in many instances is by non-mistake rather than by visible victory. Additionally, the gestation period required for new ideas to mature to profitability is often hampered by the internal accountancy disciplines of the organization. An idea, product concept or joint venture may take three to four years to mature to profitability. The normal reporting system of a business is the monthly account, followed by the quarterly report, the half-yearly review and the annual assessment. Unless such systems are intelligently interpreted, they can sound the death-knell for a slowly maturing but potentially profitable idea, and I was glad to see Hugh Davidson calling for broader measures of business performance in Chapter 2.

One answer is the venture management team, free from the shackles of the system. Quite simply, a multi-discipline venture team can bypass much bureaucracy and operate on a discrete timescale, free from monthly interruption and quarterly execution. This is not to write a blank cheque for venture managers, but it is an attempt to position them in a manner which allows imaginative distillation of new ideas, without the interference of systems which are appropriate to successful ongoing business, rather than embryonic activity.

Additionally, new business development, which I define as any new product concept, initiative or liaison which can create a new and viable profit centre for the company, should be directly account-able to the Chief Executive. This does two things:

1. It involves the Chief Planning Officer of the corporation, the Managing Director/President, in that area where planning is most important, i.e. the development of new business.
2. It elevates the whole concept of new product/new business development on the corporate totem pole, and gives a thrust and vigour to this aspect of the company's activities which it will otherwise not achieve.

From practical experience at Heinz, I can say that this structure has provided us with a rapid and apparently successful system of new business and new venture development. The drawbacks are that it is time-consuming, and for long periods of time sterile in terms of results achieved. Nevertheless, it remains among the most important responsibilities of any Chief Executive. The same is equally true of acquisitions, both in terms of defining the area of search, and in terms of participating in the negotiations for the acquisitions candidate.

Despite being an iconoclast, Hugh Davidson is old-fashioned in some of his beliefs. He believes that consumers buy product and service benefits rather than advertising or promotions. He believes the surest way to corporate growth is through product or service superiority. He believes that marketing is irrelevant unless supported by efficient low-cost operation. Additionally, he believes that all the other members of the marketing mix, such as communication, pricing and presentation, respond most amiably to a superior product and service, and will work hardest on its behalf. How many times have we all neglected this truism!

I found his book stimulating, provocative and original – or maybe it was that I was secretly flattered by his agreement with most of my pet prejudices.

Tony O'Reilly
Pittsburgh, USA, 1997

Bulletin Board

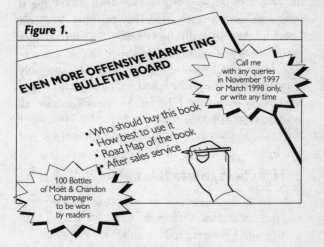

Figure 1.

EVEN MORE OFFENSIVE MARKETING
BULLETIN BOARD

Call me with any queries in November 1997 or March 1998 only, or write any time

- Who should buy this book
- How best to use it
- Road Map of the book
- After sales service

100 Bottles of Moët & Chandon Champagne to be won by readers

1. Who should buy this book

Even More Offensive Marketing is targeted at competitive people who are serious about strengthening their marketing skills and developing their career, and who are committed to Marketing as an approach to business. Its purpose is to impart practical learning, to communicate leading-edge approaches and to stimulate new thinking. Some of you will be studying Marketing, many will be practising business people. I have attempted to make the book interesting and clear to all readers. However, applying the practices and processes will require some commitment on your part, since facile shortcuts and illusory 'easy solutions' have been avoided.

I hope this book, and especially the first five chapters, will be read by Chief Executives and Board members, since Boards of Directors, not marketing people, determine whether or not their companies apply the five principles of Offensive Marketing.

2. How best to use this book

I would like everyone who buys this book to read and benefit from it. Otherwise you have wasted your money and I have wasted my time.

However, like myself, you may not read all the books you buy. Indeed, Tom Peters, joint author of *In Search of Excellence*, which sold over five million copies, estimated that only 10% of buyers read even the first five chapters.

I would therefore advise different people to use this book in different ways. Students and those taking business courses should benefit from reading the total book. Directors and senior executives are likely to find Chapters 1 to 9 most valuable, while marketing practitioners will also derive much practical advice on execution from Chapters 10 to 16.

However, it should be emphasized that *Even More Offensive Marketing* is a total package, and even if you only read a few chapters in detail, it is worth skip-reading the rest to get the full story.

3. **The Road Map of the book**

Even More Offensive Marketing is the sequel to *Offensive Marketing*, the first edition of which was published 25 years ago. While the principles of Offensive Marketing have proved enduring, the environment and techniques have obviously changed dramatically.

Even More Offensive Marketing is a new book, not a new edition. It retains the enduring principles of *Offensive Marketing* but the material is new, containing many fresh approaches and tools. It takes clear positions on issues and is deliberately practical, with many checklists, examples and step-by-step processes. Each chapter has an opening summary and a closing flow chart, and some have detailed practical exhibits at the end.

Many of the examples are taken from my own business experience, but some of these have been presented anonymously, for reasons of confidentiality. Others are fictional constructs, derived from a range of experiences. The category into which each example fits is either indicated in the text of the book or referenced.

The five key principles of Offensive Marketing – Profitable, Offensive, Integrated, Strategic and Effectively Executed, as summarized in the mnemonic POISE – have been retained, since their relevance appears to have increased over time. 'Integrated', in particular, is now very much in vogue, *though I wish people would talk less and do more about it*, and there is growing recognition of the prime importance of 'Effective Execution'.

Even More Offensive Marketing, therefore, is constructed around POISE.

Table 1.		
P: Profitable	●	Proper balance between firm's need for profit and customer's need for value
O: Offensive	●	Must lead market, take risks and make competitors followers
I: Integrated	●	Marketing approach must permeate whole company
S: Strategic	●	Probing analysis leading to a winning strategy
E: Effectively Executed	●	Strong and disciplined execution on a daily basis

Chapter 1 covers the need for Offensive Marketing, defines it and outlines its five key principles – P-O-I-S-E – which the remainder of the book develops. Here is the Road Map:

Table 2.	
P **Profitable** →	• Chapter 2 suggests that the traditional financial view of profit is outdated and describes how Offensive Marketers can develop measures of company performance more suited to contemporary business practice.
	• It shows how Offensive Marketers maximize profitability by matching their assets and competencies to the most appropriate opportunities for their companies or brands. Efficient matching of the two enables companies both to provide superior customer value and to generate superior profits.
O **Offensive** →	• Chapter 3 demonstrates the importance of vision, attitudes and values in establishing the right environment for Offensive Marketing. Even the most brilliant marketers will fail if Board attitudes towards quality, service, investment and innovation are shallow and half-hearted.

15

I **Integrated** →	• Chapter 4 is the most important in the book. It illustrates how in the Offensive Marketing company everyone is a marketer, and it outlines practical steps for making this happen.
S **Strategic** →	• 'Strategic' comprises 4 chapters, covering the main elements in preparing and developing Offensive Strategies, then translating them into effective plans. • It starts with the strategic foundation, 'Offensive Business Analysis' (Chapter 5), which outlines the requirements for effective analysis and suggests a five-step process for applying them; • Progresses to 'Developing a Distinctive View of the Future' (Chapter 6), which shows how marketers can anticipate the future and lead the development of the Strategic Plan; • And culminates in 'Developing Winning Strategies' (Chapter 7), which describes the various types of competitive advantages, and how to convert them into winning strategies. • The final chapter (Chapter 8) in the 'Strategic' section deals with turning strategies into marketing plans and incorporates an example of a fully worked plan for Rasputin Vodka.

16

E **Effectively** **Executed** →	• Chapter 9 to 15 outline how to execute Offensive Marketing Strategies and Plans. Each chapter is a mini-book, covering offensive principles governing each topic, then outlining a disciplined process for implementing them on a step-by-step basis.

	• There are seven best practice guides to:
	  ✓ Offensive Segmentation,
	  ✓ Offensive Brand Development,
	  ✓ Offensive New Product and
	    Service Development,
	  ✓ Offensive Communication,
	  ✓ Offensive Market Research,
	  ✓ Offensive Pricing,
	  ✓ Offensive Channel Management.

	• The important topic of Relationship Marketing is not given a separate chapter, since it permeates the whole of Offensive Marketing and appears in most chapters.

4. After Sales Service and Relationship Marketing

To encourage you to read the book, we have included a reader competition, with 100 prizes of Moët et Chandon champagne. You will find the entry form somewhere in the middle of the book. To enter, all you need to do is answer a few one-line questions on the book, and submit a 100–150 word example of **Even More Offensive Marketing**, either from your own experience or from published sources. All qualifying entries will be included in a random draw, to be made 25 September 1998. Your chance of winning should be pretty good, since few successful business books sell more than 10,000 copies per year, and, as you know, only a minority of readers will participate.

Finally, to reinforce my commitment to Relationship Marketing, we are setting up special phone, fax and e-mail lines in November 1997 and March 1998 only, to enable you to contact me personally to discuss any queries, criticisms or suggestions about this book. To take advantage of this opportunity, buy your copy now.

At any other time, please feel free to write to me at Penguin Books, 27 Wrights Lane, London W8 5TZ. You will of course receive a reply. I will be particularly interested to receive examples of either Offensive or Inoffensive Marketing.

I hope you feel this book has met its objectives from your viewpoint.

Hugh Davidson

1. The Offensive Marketing Approach: POISE

Chapter Summary

Marketing and Marketers are under attack. Managing and Financial Directors are questioning whether Marketing is working. They point to the lack of innovation in their companies, the high failure rate of new products, and their inability to develop sustained competitive advantage.

Marketing people in turn criticize their own companies for short-termism, unwillingness to invest or take risks, and for loading Marketing Departments with such a weight of day-to-day tactics that they have neither time nor opportunity to lead the direction of corporate strategy.

At the same time, new and old industries are enthusiastically hiring Marketing people, while the business establishment exhorts companies to adopt the marketing approach and build long-term customer relationships.

Why the paradox? Because even companies claiming to be Marketing-orientated often only go through the motions. They make aggressive noises, but continue to run on the spot with 'Me too' and 'Me three' products and services, seeking, like slimmers, magic short-term cures which require little effort. They have only a vague vision of the future, lack the determination to develop and invest in winning strategies and consistently overstate their real state of health.

This is partly because their functional structure inhibits a company-wide approach to Marketing, partly because Marketing Departments themselves often adopt a narrow and inward-looking role, failing to spearhead the company's future vision and strategy.

Yet Marketing and Marketers have never had a bigger opportunity to realize their full potential, as companies seek innovation and profitable growth, as new financial measures more favourable to Marketing, like shareholder value and the balanced scorecard, gain in popularity.

Offensive Marketing is designed to help you exploit this opportunity. It is a set of attitudes, approaches and processes practised by only a
20 handful of consistently successful companies.

Is Microsoft an Offensive Marketer?

Bill Gates was only technically a dropout when he left Harvard University in his second year. He left because, together with Paul Allen, he had developed the software language for the first personal computer, the Altair. Some of the experts at Intel, who produced the 8080 microchip for the Altair, said it was impossible to develop BASIC language for it, but Microsoft Basic was written in eight weeks, without even the benefit of an Altair computer for reference. Indeed Gates and Allen only saw a working Altair for the first time when Microsoft Word was (successfully) run on it, in Albuquerque, New Mexico.[1]

In a turbulent industry with over 75,000 competitors worldwide, and for two difficult decades, Microsoft has consistently grown sales and profits at a dramatic rate. It overtook IBM in market capitalization after only seventeen years in business.

Why has Microsoft been so successful?

Here are some reasons:[2]

- The company has a clear and easily understood vision – 'Microsoft software on every desktop PC.'
- It hires a very specific type of person with strong technical background, high intelligence, a drive to succeed and ability to handle pressure.
- It has a distinctive management style, built around informality, speed, hard challenges and stock options – directed towards making better products quickly and winning.
- Microsoft always wants to be ahead of competition in every way. It competes both in the market-place and the law courts. The drive to win is very strong.
- The company invests heavily in its vision of the future. R & D costs are 14 per cent of sales, sales/marketing investment is 32 per cent, while cost of goods is only 15 per cent of sales.

- Deal-making has always been a strength. The agreement of IBM, to use MS-DOS as the operating system in its PCs, established MS-DOS as the industry standard and enabled Microsoft to build dominance in this critical strategic area.
- Microsoft takes controlled risks and places high priority on speed to market-place.

Offensive Marketing

You have just read an example of **Offensive Marketing**. Both Microsoft and Bill Gates are Offensive Marketers.

This book is about Offensive Marketing, which combines the age-old virtues of risk-taking with a modern approach to Marketing. Offensive Marketing is practised by only a handful of successful companies, and the phrase has been coined to differentiate the contents of this book from the sluggish and specialized concept that passes for Marketing in many companies.

Offensive Marketing is not a neat concept

capable of instant encapsulation in an elegant one-liner. It describes particular attitudes and methods that cover the whole Marketing spectrum, so its boundaries are widely spread and ragged. In essence, it involves aiming to innovate every major new development in a market. It means having a clear strategy, and following it through with investment and persistence. It is about anticipating future needs, meeting them quicker and better than competition, and building strong customer relationships.

What Offensive Marketing is not

Here are some definitions to consider, serious and not so serious:

- **Marketing is a sophisticated form of selling, done by graduates**. This is what many consumers and non-business journalists think Marketing is. They believe that Marketing manipulates and exploits consumers, and pushes prices up. 'Added value' means adding more frills and doubling the price.

Marketing is not 'selling' though selling is

part of the Marketing approach. To borrow a phrase, 'Selling is making people want what you've got, while Marketing is selling people what they want.'[3] When people, and especially politicians, say, 'We must improve the Marketing of our products,' they are confusing Marketing with selling, and usually attempting to gloss over a weak customer proposition.

- **Marketing is advertising, sales promotion, selling, PR, direct mail, market research**. This is a definition rarely spoken but often followed by half-baked Marketers, whose most frequent haunts are the financial services and energy industries. Their employers think they are 'embracing' Marketing by hiring people with a Marketing title, but in reality they merely bolt on a series of marketing services to a financial or operations approach to business.
- **Marketing is what the Marketing Department does**. In many companies, that is the view of other departments, such as Operations or Finance.

This too is a narrow definition of

Marketing, for which Marketing people must take some responsibility. Ironically, most Marketers are poor communicators about Marketing.

- **Marketing is the four 'P's – Product, Price, Place and Promotion.** This is also sometimes referred to as the 'Marketing mix', and has the virtue of simplicity and clarity. 'Place' is widely viewed as distribution channels, while 'Promotion' usually includes selling and advertising as well as sales promotion.

  This definition at least recognizes that Marketing is done outside the Marketing Department, but its weaknesses are that it describes Marketing activities rather than the Marketing approach, and does not mention 'profit'.

- **The purpose of Marketing is to meet consumer needs at a profit.** The best definition yet, often used in textbooks, but unfortunately based on a sophisticated misconception.

  It fails to recognize that there may be a very real conflict between meeting consumer needs and making a profit. Every company has to do both in order to survive, but how should it strike a balance between the two? Does it aim to maximize profit, or, like many fine companies, make a 'fair' profit? Companies constantly face business choices between converting surpluses into profits or into extra consumer value, and Marketers are usually best placed to advise on the right balance.

'Meeting consumer needs *at a profit*' is therefore too vague a definition, because it ignores profit *levels*.

Why is 'Marketing' so difficult to define?

'What do you do for a living?' is a question people in Finance, Sales, Operations and even Human Resources can answer with ease at social gatherings – not so Marketing people. Two minutes of superficial conversation tail away in glazed non-comprehension. This absence of a simple explanation may be one of the reasons why the Marketing approach is so widely misunderstood, and often wrongly applied, not least by Marketing people. 27

Marketing is difficult to define and explain because it is both an approach to business practised by every employee and the name of a specific department, full of people with Marketing titles. There is constant confusion between **Marketing** and **Marketers**. 'Marketing' is no more the exclusive role of Marketers than profit is the exclusive responsibility of the Finance Department. People easily understand their financial role in helping to make profits. Yet they find it more difficult to grasp that they are also Marketers, especially if they have no direct customer contact.

This is partly because the Marketing approach is diverse and often intangible in a way that money (Finance department) or people (Human Resources) are not; and partly because Marketing people have either been too keen to appropriate credit for Marketing success, or failed to evangelize the important role every employee can play in driving the Marketing approach.

We need a new word for 'Marketing'

So, is Marketing the Marketing approach to business or the Marketing Department, or is it both?

Today the word is used colloquially to describe both, which is very confusing for everyone.

Finance has got its language right. 'Finance' describes the internal department. 'Profit' describes the financial approach to business. 'Marketing' seems a reasonable word for the internal department. But we need a totally new word to describe the Marketing approach (Table 3).

Table 3. Finance has got its language right.	
Internal department	**Approach to business**
Finance	Profits
Marketing	?

The best answer so far comes from one of my colleagues at Oxford Corporate Consultants – 'Effective Customer Value Management'. This is something which everyone, irrespective of their internal function, could accept as his or her responsibility. 'Customer', of course, covers external customers who buy products or services, and internal customers, who receive services from colleagues. 'Value' connotes the need to provide a superior mix of quality and price. And 'Management' is the process which results in customer value. The only thing missing from the definition is profitability, intrinsic, of course, to the Marketing approach. This is strongly implied in the word 'Effective', which suggests efficient and profitable delivery of customer value.

If you have better suggestions for a new phrase or word to describe the Marketing approach, please mail it to Penguin for my attention.

Offensive Marketing Defined

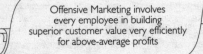

Offensive Marketing involves every employee in building superior customer value very efficiently for above-average profits

There are three key elements in this definition – not just customer focus, and profit orientation, but also cross–departmental commitment to both.

This is the *business* definition of Offensive Marketing. A separate definition for the not-for-profit or public sector is given in a later section. It does not seem possible to cover both effectively in a single definition.

'. . . **involves every employee** . . .' Every employee is a Marketer . . . whether he or she knows it or not. And if you are in the Marketing Department, it is your job to tell everyone and to recognize their contribution.

Every employee's job should be specified and evaluated on only two axes:

- Contribution to consistently superior customer value.
- Contribution to above-average profits.

What other reason is there for being in business?

Here are a couple of examples from people who never meet the customer.

- First, the **Marketing-orientated shift manager in a factory**. She is 28, has an HNC in electrical engineering and works shifts, 9 days on, 4 days off. The chart in Table 4 compares her company's factory (A) with that of her main competitor (B). Company A has no Marketing people, is more profitable and gaining market share. Company B has a Marketing Department

Table 4. A tale of two factories.	
Company A	**Company B (Competitor)**
• Buys 10% cheaper than competition via world-wide sourcing	• Efficient people with clear, though narrow objectives
• Well informed re consumer needs	• Little market knowledge
• Runs 168 hours per week, 3 shifts	• Ten 8-hour shifts, lots of overtime
• Excellent at process engineering	• Machinery and process totally undifferentiated
• Buying, sales, engineering on new product development team	• Does not leverage scale buying advantages
• Labour cost per tonne one half that of competitor's best plant	• No knowledge of competitive machinery, speeds, labour rates
• Few lines, long runs	• Many low-volume lines (SKUs)

and is losing market share. Two questions for you:

- Which company would you prefer to work for?
- Can company B be an Offensive Marketer?

The answer to the latter is 'Not for some time'. Company B would still be an Inoffensive Marketer if its Marketing Department included Bill Gates with Einstein thrown in.

Production people in a manufacturing company or Operations people in a service company are among the most important Offensive Marketers. They control the cost, quality, consistency and delivery of the customer proposition, whether it is frozen foods, insurance or consumer durables. Inefficient, high-cost operators can never be Offensive Marketers, because they cannot deliver superior consumer value at competitive profit margins.

- The second example is a **Marketing-Orientated Accountant** in the Finance

Department of an international airline. He provides accurate and timely data to all his internal customers, at reducing cost. He sticks his neck out, and forecasts future costs as well as comparing with competitors on a wide range of measures. This paragon is also working on a special project with Marketing, Sales and Operations to establish for the first time profitability by First Class, Business Class and Economy, and by type of customer (Business and Leisure).

These are examples of Offensive Marketing. The employee is *involved*. He or she understands the company vision and strategies, and knows how to help implement them. You do not need to have 'Marketing' in your title to be an Offensive Marketer.

'**. . . building . . .**' Offensive Marketers are builders, not downsizers or asset strippers. Of course they strive for efficiency and low-cost operation, so as to form a platform for superior consumer value. This, and the ability to identify growing segments and to transform markets by anticipating the future, also enables them to *build* revenue growth.

In recent years, many Western companies have pursued downsizing as a strategy, lost market share, and, for those employees retaining their jobs, become miserable places to overwork in. They get locked in a cage of reducing cost and investment, squeezing out a precarious, non-sustainable profit growth.

'. . . **superior customer value** . . .' This is achieved when *customers* recognize that you are offering a combination of quality, price and service which is superior to your competitor's proposition. The ways in which superior value can be delivered are numerous – higher quality/same price or same quality/lower price are just two of many possible gradations.

Superior customer value is difficult both to achieve and to sustain. It must be real rather than imagined, and based on objective customer measurement. Many companies say their products or services are superior, but if they have no hard evidence to prove it, they are probably deceiving 35 themselves and undermining their future in the process.

Sustaining superior value requires consistently improving performance, since every innovation is eventually successfully copied and competition is constantly moving on. Superiority should first be developed against direct competitors and then against all-comers. Customer experiences in other categories can affect your own by raising expectations. For example, speed of service at McDonalds makes customers impatient about queuing at supermarket checkouts. Faster copiers make fax machines seem very slow.

There is a virtuous circle between delivering superior customer value and profit levels: the reward for consistently superior value is high customer loyalty, and retention. Based on studies by Bain and Company, 'the companies with the highest retention rates also earn the best profits'.[4]

Everyone in business has customers. They may be colleagues inside your company, to whom you are providing a service. They may be external customers or consumers who buy your products. Whoever they are, one thing is definite. *They* are

the judges of whether you are delivering superior

value, and their view on this topic is the only one that matters.

'. . . **very efficiently** . . .' This phrase has a number of very specific meanings within the definition of Offensive Marketing. First, it means that companies need to match their strengths to the best opportunities in the market-place. Companies achieving an efficient match will have happy customers and happy shareholders. Secondly, it requires companies to be low-cost operators, with high productivity and relentless checking of whether each cost adds to customer value. Japanese companies like Toyota, Canon and Olympus are very skilful in this area, through target costing and value engineering.[5] If a company is a high-cost operator in relation to competitors, how can it possibly deliver superior value profitably?

'. . . **for above average profits** . . .' 'Above average' means better than industry norms on a range of profit measures such as return on sales (ROS), return on capital employed (ROCE) and economic value added (EVA), all of which will be reviewed in Chapter 2.

Profit is the reward earned by companies for building superior customer value very efficiently. As John Young, former CEO of Hewlett Packard, said, 'Yes, profit is a cornerstone of what we do – but it has never been the *point* in and of itself. The point, in fact, is to *win*, and winning is judged in the eyes of the consumer and by doing something you can be proud of.'[6]

Offensive Marketing is chiefly focused on generating *long-term* profit growth. If a company consistently invests in relevant new products or services, controls risk by rigorous testing of alternatives and keeps an iron hand on cost, it is likely to deliver constantly improving customer value and to enjoy both short-term and long-term profit growth.

Offensive Marketing Defined for the Not-For-Profit Sector

Offensive Marketing involves every employee in building superior customer experiences very efficiently in the most cost effective way

You will notice that this definition has much in common with the 'for business' definition of Offensive Marketing. It involves every employee; seeks superior customer satisfaction, though in terms of experience rather than value, since price is not a factor; stresses efficiency; and focuses on cost-effectiveness rather than profit.

While this book does not deal specifically with the not-for-profit or public sector, many of the approaches, processes and tools contained within it are applicable to these sectors. For charities, both definitions of Offensive Marketing may be relevant – the 'not for profit' one for fund-raising, and the 'business' one for commercial activities like retailing and mail order.

Short-term pressures facing Offensive Marketers in business

You may observe that most companies have short-term profit problems, and feel that the definition of Offensive Marketing does not address the constant tension between the short term and the long term. A question many Marketing people in business ask with feeling goes something like this:

We hear what you say about Offensive Marketing, and we would love our company, Amalgamated Leisure (AL) to adopt it. But what can we do when they say it's not affordable. Despite our protests, the company under-invests in plant, new products and new services. It has cut advertising, and our leisure attractions badly need refurbishment. Prices have been increased and we are losing customers. Our revenue is flat, but AL has increased profits by cutting more costs. We spend sixty hours a week running to stand still. Short-term profits are grossly overstated, since they contain no element of future investment.

So what is the answer? In practice, AL has no future with its current strategies. In time it will deservedly get a new owner or a new Chief Executive. This will provide an opportunity for a major profits write-down or a big reorganization charge, which will give AL the funds and breathing space to convert to Offensive Marketing . . . if it has the good sense to do so.

Offensive Marketers must hit short-term and long-term targets

While Offensive Marketing is a long-term approach, which can take years to develop fully, the reality is that Marketers have to hit short-term objectives in order to be around to enjoy the fruits of their long-term efforts.

In the short-term, Offensive Marketers need to be strong tactically and very good executors. There are many steps they can take to leverage short-term profits without mortgaging the future, and some of these are covered in Chapter 2. For the long term, they require vision and strategic skills. Marketers have to run the short term and long-term concurrently, working with both hands at the same time. This is why both strategy and execution are strongly emphasized in this book.

Clearly, Marketers have to recognize conflicts and trade-offs between the short and long-term. This section will illustrate the dilemma faced by Offensive Marketers in pursuing long-term change, and the need for patience.

The lead-times necessary to change internal attitudes and radically improve consumer value are at least two years and often longer. It is certainly not feasible within a fiscal year, and will usually reduce profits during this period, since investment will precede the revenue benefit. That is why Offensive Marketers also need to be skilled in turning up the profit meter in the short term, in order to compensate.

Table 5 illustrates by example the difference between an Offensive Marketing company and an Inoffensive Marketer in the same industry. Taking a moral tone, we will call them the Virtuous plc and the Dissembler plc.

On the face of it, both companies are making similar operating profits of 14 per cent. However, the *quality* of their profits is very different. Virtuous plc has a higher gross profit margin because its superior proposition enables it to command a premium price in the market-place. It is *investing* 23 per cent of its sales revenue in future development – in advertising, R & D and capital investment. This is clearly no guarantee of future success unless the money is wisely spent, but Virtuous plc has a superior proposition, launches successful new products, has a good innovation pipeline and
sound future prospects.

Table 5. Example: quality of profits comparison.[1]

%	Virtuous plc (%)	Dissembler plc (%)	
Sales revenue	100	100	
Cost of goods sold	43	61	
Gross profit margin	57	39	←
Advertising	11	3	
R & D	5	–	
Capital investment	7	2	
Investment ratio	23	5	←
Operating expenses	20	20	
Operating profit	14	14	
Key trends→	● Past 5-year revenue growth 10% p.a. ● Heavy advertising investment in new improved products ● Premium priced products, new plant, so low cost of goods sold	● Flat revenue, declining volume ● No recent product innovation. Little advertising ● Discounted pricing, so high cost of goods sold	

43

What about Dissembler plc, a competitor in the same industry making identical profit margins? As you can see, Dissembler is spending weakly on the future – its investment as a percentage of sales is a miserable 5% of revenue. It has unsustainable profit margins, which disguise a grisly future: a bare new product cupboard, a weakening consumer franchise and inability to finance effective R & D, plant upgrade or advertising programmes.

The table illustrates that profit viewed in isolation is a misleading measure. **For the Offensive Marketer, a more relevant measure is profit and investment as a percentage of sales**. Investment is defined as 'anything with a payback longer than one year'. This covers advertising, R & D, capital investment, training, strategic market research and most Direct Marketing (but not sales promotion, which should pay back quickly). These are the costs which many companies cut to inflate short-term profits.

Let's take one final look at Virtuous plc and Dissembler plc's profit profile before moving on. For Offensive Marketers, current-year profits will include large investment losses for new products recently launched or still in the pipeline. In other words, profits from established products will exceed total company profits (Table 6). This second perspective on Dissembler confirms that it is severely under-investing in its business, and probably faces big trouble ahead. By contrast, Virtuous's investment in tomorrow should enable it to sustain or improve on its 14% operating profit.

Table 6. The make-up of 14 per cent operating profits.		
Factor	Virtuous plc (%)	Dissembler plc (%)
Profit on existing products over 3 years old	21	15
Losses on products recently launched or in development	(7)	(1)
Total operating profits	14	14

How can Dissembler convert into a virtuous cycle? It can start by buying this book, which outlines how this can be done. However, the path will be hard and long, and it is certain that Dissembler will have to raise investment and cut profit margins. How should you react if Dissembler offers you a highly paid job? Only consider it if there is new management with the time and credibility to pursue a genuine investment strategy.

Having defined Offensive Marketing, here is a recap:

> Offensive Marketing involves
> every employee in building
> superior customer value very efficiently
> for above-average profits

I know definitions are tiresome, but this one is the lynch-pin of Offensive Marketing and the core of the remainder of the book.

How well does Microsoft meet the Offensive Marketing Definition?[8]

In the past, Microsoft has been an Offensive Marketer, although it has never employed many people with a Marketing title. Now let's check Microsoft against the Offensive Marketing definition.

'. . . **involves every employee** . . .' Microsoft employees appear to be heavily involved. They are often driven people and know in broad terms what the company is trying to achieve – speed, leadership, superiority. Although Microsoft is strong technically, it is customer driven. However, its style is often confrontational – what Bill Gates called 'high bandwidth communication' – and internal communications are less than perfect.

'. . . **Superior customer value** . . .' Microsoft's main strength has been its ability to anticipate and act upon the future now, and to constantly drive for product improvement, as summed up by three quotations:

'In our industry a disproportionate amount of economic value occurs in the early stages of a product's life . . . so there is real *value* to speed.'

– Louis Gerstner, Chairman of IBM

'One of the real keys was . . . we were always a year or two ahead of where demand was really going to be . . . and we were generally guessing right.'

– Microsoft employee

'With few exceptions, they've never shipped a good product in its first version. But they never give up, and eventually get it right.'

– Microsoft competitor

'. . . **above-average profit**.' There has never been any doubt about Microsoft's 47 performance on this score. While profit margins in PC hardware are paper-thin, Microsoft software achieves 25% net profit, and over 20% return on total assets.

Why isn't everyone an Offensive Marketer?

Since Offensive Marketing is a 'best practice' approach to Marketing, by definition few companies will fully achieve it. What is more surprising is that so few companies even attempt to climb the heights of Offensive Marketing.

Theodore Levitt's comment is still disturbingly relevant:

'When it comes to the Marketing concept today, a solid stone wall often seems to separate word and deed. In spite of the best intentions and energetic efforts of many highly able people, the effective implementation of the Marketing concept has generally eluded them.'[9]

The practice of Offensive Marketing remains the exception rather than the rule. Why?

1. **Most companies lack a distinctive vision or strategy**. The typical company rushes along from year to year in frenzied activity, without a clear vision of the future, and lacking distinctive or superior propositions. It will cut costs, undertake 'initiatives' and housekeep efficiently. It will avoid undue risks or major investments, keep a close eye on competitors so that it can remain in step and over-reward its top executives. All may be well in a normal year. But in times of major change or faced by radically new competition, this company will stumble badly, looking vainly for someone else to copy.

2. **Short-termism**. This is a well-known disorder, especially in the UK and USA, though less so in Germany or Japan. Companies are run on a fiscal year, rather than a three- to five-year basis, for the benefit of pension funds and institutions ('shareholders'). They pay more attention to security analysts than to customers. Any expenditure with a payback of over

one year will be regarded with suspicion, even hostility.

3. **Lack of understanding of the Offensive Marketing approach**. Companies either fail to grasp the importance of making customer relationships and satisfaction their central justification, or are unable to determine how to do this profitably.

4. **Lack of character**. Many companies understand the basics of the Offensive Marketing approach, but do not have the necessary qualities of courage, determination, persistence and risk-taking necessary to apply it. Offensive Marketing is less a matter of intelligence and ability – since most companies have plenty of both – than of attitudes, strategy and teamwork. It is a set of shared values, grounded in a commitment to superior consumer benefits and low-cost operation.

5. **Misguided Marketing Departments**. Conventional Marketing has often become a victim of its own success. The

acceptance of the Marketing Department has multiplied its coordination role and created floods of paper. The day-to-day pressure is so great there is no time left to innovate. In many companies the Marketing Department, far from acting as the touchstone to innovation and enterprise, has itself become a bureaucracy, spewing paper, acting as a passive coordinator.

We will return to this theme later in the chapter.

Has Marketing failed?

This question is increasingly being asked, especially by Financial Directors, and even by Managing Directors.

It sometimes hangs over discussions about long-term investments, such as R & D, advertising, new-product investment, customer service improvements or long-term warranties, all of which tend to be associated with Marketing. While few would disagree with the theory of the Marketing approach, many would question the cost and efficiency with which it has been implemented.

Arguments used by a Finance Director might include the following:

1. ' **"Marketing" is not giving us a clear view of the future**. We spend a lot of money on consumer research, but it seems to tell us little about the future. Consumers can't articulate their future needs or priorities, especially if they know less than we do about tomorrow's technology and the vistas it will open. I'm concerned that the glut of information we have about the past is clogging our entrepreneurial arteries.' (Yes, some enlightened Finance Directors think like this.)

2. '**We're constantly being surprised and outflanked by our competitors**. They seem to be getting to market quicker with new products, and we spend our time running to catch up. We have a big new-product development programme, but the failure rate of new products is still

incredibly high, and we even go national with new programmes which haven't been fully tested. We're always on the back foot.'

3. **'I am not convinced that Marketing-orientated companies are necessarily the most profitable**. Some of the most profitable companies in recent years have been built up via acquisitions, deals, low operating costs and speed of reaction. There is nothing special about their products or services, but the companies are run by entrepreneurs.'

4. **'We spend a vast amount on advertising, but I question the means used to evaluate it**. Marketers, aided by their advertising agencies, always say we are underspending, but can't even justify the present level of expenditure.'

5. **'I notice that the fast-moving consumer goods companies which originated Marketing seem to have lost the initiative to retailers**. Many of them appear to be struggling in mature markets with undistinctive brands and

some are producing low-margin private label products for retailers just to survive. What on earth can they teach us?'

What do you think of these arguments and which are most effective? Are they fair? Table 7 shows an objective top-line response.

Perhaps the most decisive sign that 'Marketing works' is the speed with which the Marketing approach has spread to almost every industry, from financial services to leisure, from automobiles to copiers, from airlines to accountancy, from stately homes to metal piping.

Few people today would argue with a business model that focuses on two major linked objectives – minimizing cost and maximizing customer value. Many of the apparent criticisms of Marketing, as you will already have observed, are in fact implied criticisms of Marketers or Marketing Departments.

Table 7.	
Question	**Response**
1. 'Marketing is not giving us a clear view of the future.'	This is a matter for the Board, following the Marketing approach. Your points about research and data-glut are well made.

Question	Response
2. 'We're constantly being surprised and outflanked by our competitors.'	This is because you are following not leading. However, your point about the high failure rate of new products is a powerful indictment of 'Marketers'.
3. 'I am not convinced that Marketing-orientated companies are necessarily the most profitable.'	An increasing body of academic research, and the PIMS (profit impact of Marketing strategy) studies suggest that companies with a strong customer orientation achieve above-average profit margins and growth in the long term.
4. 'We spend a vast amount on advertising, but I question the means used to evaluate it.'	Tools to evaluate advertising have improved greatly in recent years. It sounds as if your company is not using them.
5. 'I notice that the fast-moving consumer goods companies which originated Marketing seem to have lost the initiative to retailers.'	They tend to be in mature markets like food or household goods. The originators of Marketing – companies like Procter & Gamble, Unilever, Colgate, SmithKline Beecham, Mars and Nestlé, continue to do well. Many of their followers in food and household goods are struggling.

Have Marketers failed Marketing?

A critical view. Table 8 gives a chart from a presentation to a blue-chip company with a long-established Marketing Department.

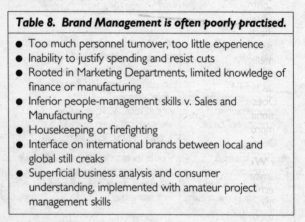

> ### Table 8. Brand Management is often poorly practised.
>
> - Too much personnel turnover, too little experience
> - Inability to justify spending and resist cuts
> - Rooted in Marketing Departments, limited knowledge of finance or manufacturing
> - Inferior people-management skills v. Sales and Manufacturing
> - Housekeeping or firefighting
> - Interface on international brands between local and global still creaks
> - Superficial business analysis and consumer understanding, implemented with amateur project management skills

At this presentation no one walked out. Nobody complained. There were few questions at the end and much agreement.

A balanced view. Table 9 evaluates the past performance of Marketers by a Managing Director, drafted in the form of a simplified personnel 56 appraisal form.

Table 9. Marketing Department: Appraisal Form

Name: *Marketing Department*
Appraised by: *Managing Director*

Key Strengths:

1. Contribution to consumer-driven long term business strategy.
2. Effective coordination of business activities on brand basis, across departments.
3. Intelligent, highly motivated people who work hard.
4. Runs communications function reasonably well, though has difficulty justifying expenditure levels.
5. Does good job in identifying existing consumer needs, monitoring competitive position and developing improvement plans.
6. Department role well accepted across the company.

Key Weaknesses

1. Limited knowledge of and interest in operations or technology.
2. Planning, forecasting and project management skills below standard.
3. Performance on new product development disappointing, with low output of genuine innovations, high failure rate.
4. Business analysis and financial skills insufficient.
5. Inability to spot new opportunities early, or to correctly anticipate change – spends too much time catching up.
6. Fails to evangelize the marketing approach across the company.
7. Lacks the data to win arguments within the board about long-term investment and does not fight hard enough.

So, are Marketing Departments necessary?

Looking at this appraisal form, which some may consider generous to Marketers, you may wonder whether Marketing Departments are needed. Religions can flower without churches, or even, as the Quakers have shown, without priests. Marks & Spencer, a strong exponent of superior customer value and high profit margins, has succeeded for a hundred years without a Marketing Department (although it has a Marketing Services Department). Mercedes, with a distinctive and premium-priced product range, and good margins by car industry standards, only started its Marketing Department three years ago. Many Japanese companies manage successfully without specialist Marketers, but any Marketer would point out that their profit margins are often in low single figures, and their record in building shareholder value is poor, in recent years.

There are only a limited number of Western companies successfully applying the Marketing approach without the help of a Marketing Department, and few are disbanded. There are sound reasons for having them, and here are the main ones:

1. **Double perspective**. The Marketing Department is the only one with a clear view of external customer needs and internal company skills. The ability to understand and match these is critical to business success (Figure 2).

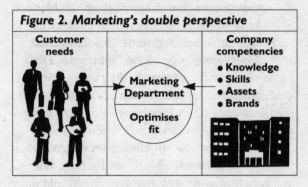

Figure 2. Marketing's double perspective

Customer needs

Marketing Department

Optimises fit

Company competencies
- Knowledge
- Skills
- Assets
- Brands

Finance and Human Resource departments have a bird's-eye view of the internal workings of a company, but little knowledge of customers and their needs, so their perspective is one-dimensional.

2. **Strategy and planning input**. Successful company strategies start by defining future market and customer needs.

59

They then target those needs which their particular competencies enable them to meet in a superior way. Marketing people are well placed to set and lead this strategic agenda, because of their familiarity with market needs, their ability to forecast future trends and their objective knowledge of company competencies.

3. **Market and segment prioritization**. Marketers can advise which markets and market segments have most future attraction, which should be dropped, and how resources should be allocated across markets and brands.

4. **Coordination and long-term project management**. Most major improvements and innovations involve wide cross-departmental co-operation, and frequently include many external agencies. The Marketing Department can coordinate proactively, using business planning processes, especially on multi-country or global projects.

5. **Category and Brand Management**. Someone needs to develop, plan and

monitor the day-to-day business, with eyes fixed on the customer. Depending on the type of business, this will include tasks like sales forecasting, customer service, support programmes, results monitoring, analysing competitive activity and so on.

6. **Expertise**. Marketing people should possess specialized competencies, such as:

- Ability to anticipate future customer needs, through knowledge of market and technology trends
- Skill in value-analysing use of resources – for example, assessing the customer value of the various elements in a product or service and relating each of these to their cost.
- Business analysis and strategy development.
- Management and motivation of people, over whom they have no line authority.
- Skill in identifying opportunities and allocating resources to areas of best return.

In summary, then, the Marketing Department has a potentially very important and unique role. However, Marketers spend the vast majority of their time on day-to-day operations and (often unwillingly) neglect longer-term issues such as strategy development and innovation. They also change jobs much too often. If Marketing Departments are to meet their potential in future, these issues must be tackled head-on.

The future is Offensive Marketing

Offensive Marketing is a set of attitudes, principles and processes which release the potential of the Marketing approach to transform businesses. It is designed to make your competitors followers. Offensive Marketing is not a formula, a fad or an academic theory. It is a demanding and practical approach to business, which requires courage, persistence and determination. That is the reason why it is practised by only a minority of companies.

There are five elements in the Offensive Marketing approach, and these form the structure of this book. They are Profitable, Offensive,

Integrated, Strategic and Effectively Executed, summarized by the mnemonic POISE (Table 10).

Table 10.		
P:	*Profitable*	● *Proper balance between firm's needs for profit and customer's need for value*
O:	*Offensive*	● *Must lead market, take risks and make competitors followers*
I:	*Integrated*	● *Marketing approach must permeate whole company*
S:	*Strategic*	● *Probing analysis leading to a winning strategy*
E:	*Effectively Executed*	● *Strong and disciplined execution on a daily basis*

POISE spelt slowly

Let us take a look at the individual ingredients of Offensive Marketing in broad terms:

Profitable: The object of Marketing is not just to increase market share or to provide good value for consumers, but to increase profit. Offensive Marketers will encounter conflicts between giving consumers what they want and running the company efficiently. One of their skills is to reach the right balance between these sometimes opposing elements.

Offensive: An offensive approach calls for an attitude of mind which decides independently what is best for a company, rather than waiting for competition to make the first move.

Integrated: Where Marketing is integrated, it permeates the whole company. It challenges all employees to relate their work to the needs of the market-place and to balance it against the firm's profit needs.

Strategic: Winning strategies are rarely developed without intensive analysis and careful consideration of alternatives. A business operated on a day-to-day basis, with no long-term Marketing purpose, is more likely to be a follower than a leader.

Effectively Executed: No amount of intelligent approach work is of any use without effective execution. Effective execution is not just a matter of good implementation by Marketing people. It is also vitally dependent on the relationship between Marketing and other departments, and on how far common strategies and objectives exist.

How Marketers Can Spearhead Offensive Marketing

To be effective in future, and to respond purposefully to justified criticism, Marketing Departments and Marketers will need to change radically in the next few years. Best-practice Marketers are already moving forward on five fronts.

1. Structure

In mature Marketing Departments, line Marketing people frequently spend 80–90 per cent of their time on short-term tactical activity. In new ones, they often have a service role, focusing on Marketing activities. The result is that Marketers often fail to lead the development of corporate strategy, a role they are ideally qualified to spearhead because of their double perspective. The vacuum is often filled by Finance people, inadequately, because they only have a single perspective.

To remedy this, Marketers need to do two things. First, restructure Marketing Departments so that the most gifted line Marketers have time to think about strategy and win the future. In

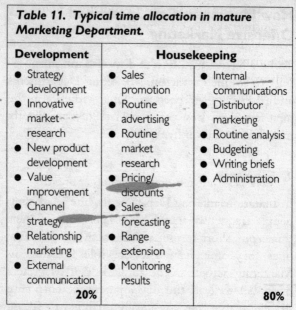

Table 11. Typical time allocation in mature Marketing Department.

Development	Housekeeping	
• Strategy development • Innovative market research • New product development • Value improvement • Channel strategy • Relationship marketing • External communication	• Sales promotion • Routine advertising • Routine market research • Pricing/discounts • Sales forecasting • Range extension • Monitoring results	• Internal communications • Distributor marketing • Routine analysis • Budgeting • Writing briefs • Administration
20%		**80%**

Source: Oxford Corporate Consultants Client Surveys

particular, contract back inessential administration to other departments wherever possible – one Marketer's comment is indicative, 'I think often in my organization, Marketing is a "skip".'[10]

Secondly, Marketers need to transform their relationships with other departments, whose efforts are critical to the success of Offensive Marketing. It is remarkable how inward-looking Marketers can be. They spend vast amounts of time attending seminars on how to get the best out of their advertising agencies, but give little thought to the much more important issue of how to get the best out of other departments, like Finance, Sales and Operations. This merits more attention and will be fully addressed in Chapter 4 on Integration. Above

Table 12. Time allocation by contact point.		
Contact point		**% of time**
External agencies	*Advertising, direct Marketing, packaging, research, sales promotion*	26%
Others within Marketing Department	*Colleagues up, down, across*	26%
On own in office	*Analysis, planning, coordination, administration*	25%
Other departments (Sales, Operations, etc.)	*Routine 18% strategic 2%*	20%
With customers or consumers		3%

Source: Author's estimate

all, Marketers need to spend more time talking to customers and consumers (Table 12).

The need within Marketing Departments to separate development from housekeeping has become obvious. One way to achieve this is by having Brand Equity Managers, with overall responsibility for business performance but primary focus on managing the six development drivers capable of dramatically improving competitive position (Table 13).

Table 13. The six marketing development drivers.

1. Deep understanding of consumer needs and habits, and awareness of likely future changes in markets and technology.
2. Strategy and portfolio management, setting tomorrow's agenda for the whole company
3. Product and service development
4. Prioritizing and monitoring investment in plant, service improvements and consumer relationships.
5. Marketing Value Analysis – looking at every product or service cost and relating it to consumer benefit
6. Actively managing the marketing approach across departments, and identifying key company competencies to be exploited.

Housekeeping – important tasks like sales forecasting, distributor or trade marketing, sales promotion, direct marketing and routine communication – can be handled by specialists in a central service department, working closely with Brand Equity Managers. Figure 3 shows how this approach to Marketing organization could work in a hotel company, using Marketing Equity people to manage the six key development drivers.

In recent years, Marketing Services have been downsized or dispensed with altogether. The result has been to overload line Marketing Executives so that only the short term gets done. There is a need to increase the number of service specialists to enable the Brand Equity Managers to develop the future, the task they are best qualified to do. People in Marketing Services have two potential career paths – becoming long-term specialists or moving to Brand Equity management.

While in some companies this would lead to an increase in the number of Marketing people, in others the new structure would generate greater efficiency from existing people, by allocating them to areas best suited to their skills, by adopting more disciplined process management (see figure

Figure 3. Illustration: marketing department of hotel company.

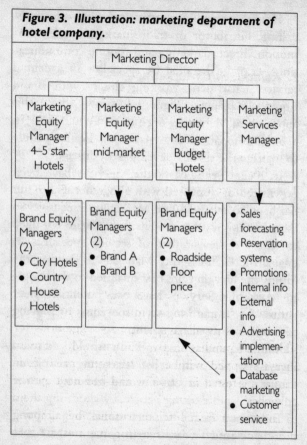

3) and by leveraging information more effectively through IT.

2. Relationship Marketing

One of the biggest future opportunities for Marketers is leadership in further developing Relationship Marketing.

In the days before most readers of this book were born, local shopkeepers relied strongly on it. Their product range, brands stocked and pricing were usually similar to competitors, and Relationship Marketing was the key differentiator. This involved understanding the specific needs of each customer, and meeting them exactly. For instance, Mrs Jones liked her bacon streaky and thinly cut, and enjoyed a good chat, especially about her dogs. She wasn't very price conscious, wanted to buy the best and was usually responsive to suggestions for additional purchases. By contrast, Mrs Brown always shopped with a list, was very price conscious, interested in bargains and had no time for 'idle chat'.

Today, as a frequent international flier arriving at a check-in desk, you may (or may not) be told 71 that as usual you have been booked a non-smoker aisle seat, a vegetarian meal, are in line for an upgrade from Business Class to First Class, and may be interested in a frequent flier 'spouse' offer to Rome next month. In this case, the airline has used your database derived from past requests and purchase habits to offer you an individualized travel experience.

Relationship Marketing represents a future opportunity not just to Marketers of high ticket items like cars, credit cards and financial services, but also to fast-moving consumer goods marketers. Why else does Procter & Gamble have a consumer database of 44 million households in the USA (and 7 million plus in the UK), with Kraft a close second at 40 million? Of course, the quality of these databases will vary widely, and, like many emerging areas, Relationship Marketing is prone to hype.

However, a number of important factors will continue to drive its growth:

Falling costs of IT. In the past few years, cost of holding and developing consumer databases has dived, and will continue to do so. Telecom costs are also declining, though not nearly so steeply.

Feasibility of building high-quality databases. Companies can build their own through mailings, questionnaires and promotions, buy them in from specialist operators, or, as usually happens, do both. Some of these databases contain quite detailed information, like type and age of car, size and neighbourhood of house, pets owned, frequency and location of holidays, and so on. In the USA, Donnelly's complete database includes 87 million of the 95 million households in the country, and many of these have answered seventy questions.[11]

Growing sophistication of consumers. As every Marketer knows, today's consumers are very much in the driving seat. They have strong bargaining power, often buy in markets with surplus capacity, and can become overwhelmed with an excess of choice. Consumers have also learned the lessons of the recession years, seek superior value, and want to be treated as individuals, not as anonymous numbers or mass-market fodder.

Response by Marketers to consumer trends. Modern Relationship Marketing views customers as potential long-term income streams, not as 'one-off' selling opportunities. Marketers of fast-moving consumer goods have always recognized this instinctively. They know that the cost of generating a single sale is uneconomic, and that the success of any brand depends on its ability to achieve repeat purchase. However, by heavily price promoting parity products, thereby investing in large numbers of price-driven brand switchers, they have often failed to translate this logic into reality.

Some of the new Marketers, in categories like eating out, retailing, software, telecom and insurance, have led the way in Relationship Marketing. They have developed high-quality databases, containing information on demographics, life stage, lifestyle and past purchases, and used these to build relationships. First Direct Bank is one of the best practitioners. Many Relationship Marketers also use loyalty cards and clubs to both provide incentives and gain further information.

A further reason why Relationship Marketing appeals to companies is the opportunity it gives to make direct contact with the customer, and so remove reliance on intermediaries. This is funda-
mentally changing distribution channel marketing.

Improved measurement of customer economics. Two valuable tools in Relationship Marketing are long-term customer profit and share of customer.

Long-term customer profit involves calculating how long you are likely to retain a particular customer, estimating value of purchases less cost of retention over that period, and adding on a bonus for customer referrals. These calculations are sometimes referred to as lifetime customer value (LCV). Knowing LCV can guide you on how much to spend on customer retention, and how much on gaining new customers.

Various studies have demonstrated not only the obvious point that existing customers are more profitable than new ones, but also that companies tend to under-invest in existing customers. One of the best studies shows that, across a number of markets, *a 5% increase in annual customer retention can increase total company operating profits by over 50%*.[12] It illustrates that existing loyal customers are by far the most valuable because they:

- Involve no business acquisition cost.
- Buy a broader range of products due to familiarity with the company's total product line.

- Cost less to service, through understanding the company's business system and using it efficiently.

- Recommend products to other customers.

The One to One Future[13] claims that most businesses lose 25% of their customers annually, **and yet most companies spend *six times* as much on generating new customers as on retaining existing ones**. I'm tempted to repeat that. Think about it carefully.

Assuming you avoid this trap, and achieve a high customer retention rate, 'share of customer' is another valuable measure to consider. It should supplement 'share of market', not replace it. 'Share of customer' indicates the depth of commitment each customer has to you, and charts your opportunity to increase revenue among existing customers.

'Share of customer is the brand's market share of the individual.'[14] To take a simple example, heavy credit card users in the USA carry 6.2 cards: **What is your share of total credit card spending among these heavy users, and is it increasing or decreasing**? Clearly, it is important to define
the competitive framework. For instance, in the

above example, should you include short-term borrowing from banks in your 'share of customer'?

'Share of customer', especially among heavy users, is also an important measure in fast-moving consumer goods. Together with loyalty, it indicates the level of commitment to your brand, when compared with competitors, on a trend basis. Brands with low loyalty scores and poor share of customer will decline, even though supported by a steadily increasing series of price reductions, which may even speed up their journey to oblivion.

Ability to develop tailored products and services economically. Although the move by manufacturers to mass customization has been greatly exaggerated, techniques to tailor products efficiently on a low-volume basis are certainly improving. This is particularly apparent in the car industry, where each basic model has scores of options. Stoves, a cooker manufacturer, offers consumers in Germany a wide menu of alternatives, allows them to construct their own cooker and aims to deliver within two weeks. Cost of a tailored version is about 10% more than an 'off-the-shelf' cooker.[15]

However, this trend should be viewed with caution. Set against the growing *capability* to customize products is the reality that high volume manufacture of a limited range of items should always be more efficient. Recognizing the consumer desire for better value, and the trade-off between price and choice, many leading manufacturers are deliberately cutting unnecessary choice, in setting up low-cost pan-European manufacturing sites. One has a ten-year plan to reduce its number of product varieties in Europe from 2000 to 200, in its quest to improve consumer value, by driving down price in real terms.

Services are usually much easier to tailor economically to the needs of groups or individuals, especially as IT costs decline.

Fragmentation of media. The increasing cost of mass media, especially TV, makes it affordable and effective only for larger brands. How to market secondary brands efficiently has become a big issue for Marketers. Relationship Marketing has a part to play in the solution. At the same time, media is becoming more customized with the growth of specialist TV channels and magazines, so offering further opportunities for tightly targeted Relationship Marketing.

This brief review of Relationship Marketing is designed to highlight its importance as a spearhead and opportunity for Offensive Marketers in the future. It influences every aspect of Marketing, but especially strategy, integration, allocation of resources, segmentation, branding, communication, and channels.

3. Competency development

At present, some Marketers lack the necessary skills to be effective in today's environment, and these deficiencies will become cruelly exposed in future.

Tomorrow's Marketer needs to be:

- Knowledgeable about the essentials of operations, the supply chain and channel management
- Able to understand the key technologies of the business
- Literate in finance and IT
- Skilful in project planning and management

- A first-class business analyst, using data objectively and creatively to develop succinct action plans
- A skilful manager and motivator of the scores of people, inside and outside the company, who help implement the Marketing approach
- Expert in opportunity identification, market research, advertising strategy and evaluation, direct marketing, customer service, etc.

This inventory of required skills is much broader than today's typical specification of a Marketer. If Marketers are truly to help realize the full potential of the Marketing approach, more will have formal Marketing qualifications, and be drawn from technical and financial as well as arts backgrounds. Yesterday's profile of the Marketer with an arts degree, a cavalier lack of interest in technology and operations and weak project management skills, will become irrelevant tomorrow.

Table 14 summarizes today's and tomorrow's required Marketing Department competencies. There will be a move from Marketing manage-

Table 14. Marketers' competencies.	
Today:	**Tomorrow:**

● Business analysis
● Innovation
● Project management
● Coordination
● IT skills
● Strategic skills
● Cost management
● Consumer understanding
● Marketing techniques
	● Today's, plus
	  ○ Financial skills
	  ○ Technology knowledge
	  ○ Database marketing
	  ○ Cross-department leadership
	  ○ Operations know-how
	  ○ Corporate strategy
	  ○ Alliances and acquisitions

Marketing management	*Corporate business management*

ment to corporate business management, as the table demonstrates.

Marketers will need to develop both today's and tomorrow's skills. These skills should be put in context. For instance, in Finance or Operations, Marketers will not be expected to build new costing or inventory control systems, since these are specialized skills. But they will be expected to 81 understand the basic principles, so that they can ask intelligent questions and specify their needs. Despite this qualification, you may still argue that this list of Marketers' competencies looks like a list for General Management. This is no coincidence – tomorrow's Marketers will become increasingly well-equipped for General Management.

4. Marketing process management

For many years, people in Operations and Selling, and, to some degree, Finance, have followed process management. Their activities have been divided into a series of processes, which are clearly understood and can be equally accurately evaluated.

For example, Operations people may be assessed on number of transactions, or units produced, quality, timeliness, customer service levels and cost. Sales people are measured by revenue, cost of sales, quality of relationships and, in the case of a field sales force, interviews, orders per day, distribution, service levels and so on.

All these activities are evaluated quantitatively, either fully or in part. Performance can be compared with objectives and previous year, across other company business units or countries, or even benchmarked against external companies. And most of these Selling or Operations activities are executed in a disciplined way, following prescribed sequences, which have been developed and refined over the years.

Marketers seem to have escaped all this. Ask a McDonald's manager what he plans to do tomorrow and he will tell you precisely what he expects to accomplish – perhaps £4,600 revenue, with eight full-time and six part-time staff, at a cost of X, in fourteen trading hours. Ask any Marketing people what they plan to do tomorrow, and the answers will vary widely, a mishmash of meetings, phone calls, writing and paper pushing.

And how will they do it? Do they have an agreed 'best way' of doing things, like the McDonald's manager, with his procedure book? Probably not. Even within companies, they often approach the processes of new product development, advertising evaluation, opportunity identification and a whole host of tasks in different ways, if indeed they use formal process management at all.

And how do Marketers evaluate their business performance? Market share?

'Yes, our market share has declined, but we were heavily out-advertised by competition, and anyway our profits have grown this year because we cut spending and increased prices.'

Innovation? This is hard to measure, and lead-times are long, while Marketing people change jobs or assignments frequently. Quality of advertising?

'Well, our advertising awareness shot up this year. No, sales didn't increase . . . we're not sure why.'

Marketers have managed to escape most of the rigours of accountability and the disciplines of process management, because their activities are diverse, often hard to predict, and difficult to measure. Disciplines have often been resisted because they 'stifle creativity'. Marketers tend to be very articulate people, and some would rather operate on the qualitative high ground of intuition and judgement than on the plebeian territory of boring quantitative evaluation.

This is all going to change, and rapidly. Marketing is becoming more scientific, more accountable and more process driven. The best Marketers are leading the way, and Managing

Directors, with Financial Directors at their side, will insist that this change takes place.

Table 15 summarizes key changes in Marketing management style.

Table 15. Future changes in Marketing management style.			
	Yesterday	**Today**	**Tomorrow**
Style	Seat of pants	Marketing planning	Strategic Process Management
Accountability	Low	Medium	High
Measurability	Low	Medium	High
Orientation	Focus on Marketing Dept and Agencies	Cross departmental coordination	Cross departmental management

The majority of this book – Chapters 5 to 15 – is concerned with developing winning strategies and executing them. It will treat these topics creatively yet scientifically, covering principles then processes.

5. Priorities

Changes in Marketing structures, competencies required and a more disciplined process-driven management style will all provide Marketers with the opportunity to make a quantum leap in effectiveness. They will also lead to new priorities (Table 16).

Table 16. Future priorities for Marketing Departments.

Priorities	How
Corporate strategy business development	• New structures • New competencies • Cross-departmental focus
Broaden competencies	• Widen personnel selection criteria • Build technical, IT, financial skills among Marketers • Rotate people across departments
Evangelize Marketing approach across company	• Regular market reports in readable form for all depts • Invite other managers to Sales Meetings, Away Days • Enhance motivating skills of Marketers
Strengthen Marketing's leadership role	• Finance and Operations Managers to make regular field visits • Marketers to identify and exploit companies' key skills
More outward-facing Marketing Departments	• Marketing people to spend more time with customers and Operations people • Marketers to give others full credit for Marketing successes

Above all, Marketers need to encourage everyone in the company to talk to customers, as do the Japanese: 'The Japanese have long considered Marketing a business for everyone in the company, not a professional pursuit of some specialists, and Japanese engineers, designers and top managers have a tradition of participating in sales efforts, Marketing research and service calls.'[16]

Sustainability of Offensive Marketing

While it will be difficult and challenging for Dissembler plc to become an Offensive Marketer, Virtuous plc and Microsoft will not remain Offensive Marketers for ever.

Companies which have failed to adopt Offensive Marketing include most banks, petroleum companies, insurers, department stores, utilities and railways, and many automobile companies.

However, it is certainly easier to remain an Offensive Marketer than to become one, because every Offensive Marketer carries forward the momentum of accumulated past investment, successful risk-taking and purposeful strategies. 87

The primary traps for Offensive Marketers are misreading of future needs and complacency. IBM fell victim to both:

IBM's first major setback was the failure of its PC in the late 1970s, and while it continued to generate annual net profits of $5 billion to $6 billion through the 1980s, it lost momentum.

In 1991–3, IBM lost $16 billion, but in 1990 when net profit was $6 billion, the Annual Report sighted no hurricanes on the horizon. Here are some quotations from it:

- **'The future of large computers is one of continued healthy growth.'**
- **'Our strategy is straightforward and consistent:**
  - **to provide customers with the best solutions**
  - **to strengthen the competitiveness of our products and services**
  - **to improve our efficiency.'**
- **'We are offering the strongest line-up of products and services in our history.'**

Few Annual Reports of any description contain as many references to 'customers' as IBM's in 1990 before the earthquake struck.

Some years later, Louis Gerstner, IBM's current Chairman, observed:

'At the heart of the turmoil is one simple fact: IBM failed to keep pace with significant change in the industry.

'We have been too bureaucratic and too preoccupied with our view of the world. We have been too slow getting things to market.'

Within a few short years, IBM moved from bluest of blue chips to virtual basket case. For years it had hired the cream of the graduate crop. The company had a powerful internal culture, which drove performance but not change. Its R & D Department boasted a number of Nobel prize winners, and virtually invented the computer industry, but became preoccupied with technology rather than superior consumer value. IBM had vast resources, but misread the

future, underinvesting in software and PCs. It was let down by poor Marketing. However, IBM may well become an Offensive Marketer under Gerstner.

Some companies have successfully sustained Offensive Marketing, based on the definition earlier in the chapter, for many years, such as those in Table 17.

While many Japanese companies, such as Honda, Sony, Fujitsu and Toyota, do excellently in generating superior consumer experiences, their low margins and inconsistent profit record in recent years exclude them from the list.

Table 17. Long-term Offensive Marketers.	
Coca-Cola	Canon
Marks & Spencer	Johnson & Johnson
BMW	SmithKline Beecham
Procter & Gamble	3M
McKinsey	Unilever
British Airways	Walt Disney

Checking a company's score for Offensive Marketing

If Offensive Marketing is as practical a concept as has been claimed, it should be possible to set up criteria by which the Offensive Marketing rating of a firm can be judged. Like any comparison between firms, the result will inevitably be biased and subjective due to differences in definition and market situations. The battery of Offensive Marketing yardsticks which has been constructed will not escape these criticisms, but they contain sufficient objectivity to be useful (Table 18, following page).

Table 18. Criteria for rating a business on Offensive Marketing.

	Max. score	Your score
Strong and differentiated customer proposition	15	
Ability to anticipate and act on future trends quickly	8	
Success in launching profitable new products/ services which add incremental sales	7	
New markets successfully entered in past ten years	7	
Strong customer focus of total company, including Operations, Distribution and Finance	15	
Strong profit focus of whole company, including Marketing and Sales	10	
Clear long-term strategy led by Marketing	8	
Commitment to constant improvement in quality and value for money	10	
More efficient/lower cost operator than competitors	12	
Level of investment compared with competitors (facilities, databases, technology, advertising, R & D, people development)	8	
Total	**100**	

FLOW-CHART SUMMARY OF CHAPTER 1

1 **Offensive Marketing defined**
- Involves every employee
- Builds superior customer value
- Above-average profits

2 **Barriers to Offensive Marketing**
- No distinctive vision or strategy
- Short-termism
- Lack of courage, determination
- Misguided Marketing Departments

3 **Criticism of Marketing and Marketers**
- Planning, forecasting, project management weak
- Failure rate of new products
- Poor reading of future change
- Weak financial, analytical skills
- Inability to justify investment spending

4 **Marketing Departments have important role**
- Double perspective
- Consumer-driven corporate strategy
- Special expertise
- Project management
- Coordination

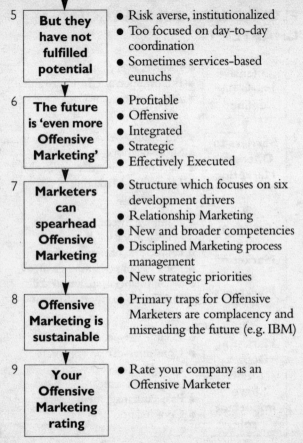

5	**But they have not fulfilled potential**	• Risk averse, institutionalized • Too focused on day-to-day coordination • Sometimes services-based eunuchs
6	**The future is 'even more Offensive Marketing'**	• Profitable • Offensive • Integrated • Strategic • Effectively Executed
7	**Marketers can spearhead Offensive Marketing**	• Structure which focuses on six development drivers • Relationship Marketing • New and broader competencies • Disciplined Marketing process management • New strategic priorities
8	**Offensive Marketing is sustainable**	• Primary traps for Offensive Marketers are complacency and misreading the future (e.g. IBM)
9	**Your Offensive Marketing rating**	• Rate your company as an Offensive Marketer